Artful Snacks

by Marilyn LaPenta

Consultant:
Sharon Richter, MS, RD, CDN

BEARPORT
PUBLISHING

NEW YORK, NEW YORK

Credits

All food illustrations by Kim Jones

Publisher: Kenn Goin
Senior Editor: Lisa Wiseman
Creative Director: Spencer Brinker
Design: Debrah Kaiser

Library of Congress Cataloging-in-Publication Data

LaPenta, Marilyn.
  Artful snacks / by Marilyn LaPenta ; consultant, Sharon Richter.
    p. cm. — (Yummy tummy recipes)
  Includes bibliographical references and index.
  ISBN-13: 978-1-61772-307-0 (library binding)
  ISBN-10: 1-61772-307-X (library binding)
1. Snack foods—Juvenile literature. 2. Cookbooks—Juvenile literature. 3. Cooking—Juvenile literature. I. Title.
  TX740.L26 2012
  641.5'3—dc23
                      2011019695

For more information, write to Bearport Publishing Company, Inc., 45 West 21st Street, Suite 3B, New York, New York 10010. Printed in the United States of America in North Mankato, Minnesota.

073011
042711CGE

10 9 8 7 6 5 4 3 2 1

Contents

Making Artful Snacks

Get ready to make some of the yummiest snacks you'll ever put in your tummy! The delicious recipes in *Artful Snacks* are super easy to make. Many of them come with ideas for creating treats that are visually interesting as well as tasty. Once you make a recipe, try your own ideas for making the snack look like a work of art!

The great thing about making your own food is that you know exactly what goes into it. When you make your own snacks, for example, you can carefully choose healthy ingredients. You can limit items with **preservatives**, which are not always good for your body. You can also choose **low-fat** dairy products instead of full-fat items to make your snacks more heart healthy. Too many calories, especially from foods high in fat or sugar, may lead to **obesity**. Use the ideas on page 22 for making the healthy snacks in this cookbook even more nutritious.

Getting Started

Use these cooking and safety tips, as well as the tool guide, to make the best snacks you've ever tasted.

Tips

Here are a few tips to get your cooking off to a great start.

- Quickly check out the Prep Time, Tools, and Servings information at the top of each recipe. It will tell you how long the recipe takes to prepare, the tools you'll need, and the number of people the recipe serves.

- Once you pick a recipe, set out the tools and ingredients that you will need on your worktable.

- Before and after cooking, wash your hands well with warm soapy water.

- Wash fruits and vegetables with edible skins before using them in the recipes.

- Put on an apron or a smock to protect your clothes.

- Roll up long shirtsleeves to keep them clean.

- Tie back or cover long hair to keep it out of the food.

- *Very important*: Keep the adults happy by cleaning up the kitchen when you've finished cooking.

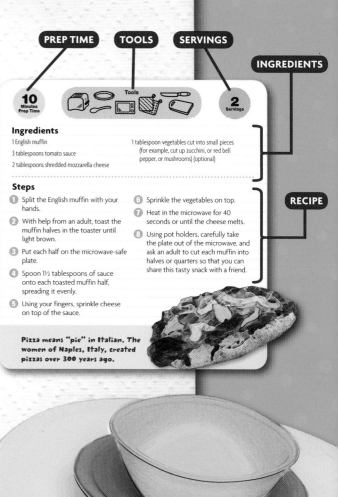

PREP TIME   **TOOLS**   **SERVINGS**   **INGREDIENTS**

10 Minutes Prep Time   Tools   **2** Servings

Ingredients

1 English muffin

3 tablespoons tomato sauce

2 tablespoons shredded mozzarella cheese

1 tablespoon vegetables cut into small pieces (for example, cut up zucchini, or red bell pepper, or mushrooms) (optional)

Steps   **RECIPE**

1. Split the English muffin with your hands.
2. With help from an adult, toast the muffin halves in the toaster until light brown.
3. Put each half on the microwave-safe plate.
4. Spoon 1½ tablespoons of sauce onto each toasted muffin half, spreading it evenly.
5. Using your fingers, sprinkle cheese on top of the sauce.
6. Sprinkle the vegetables on top.
7. Heat in the microwave for 40 seconds or until the cheese melts.
8. Using pot holders, carefully take the plate out of the microwave, and ask an adult to cut each muffin into halves or quarters so that you can share this tasty snack with a friend.

Pizza means "pie" in Italian. The women of Naples, Italy, created pizzas over 300 years ago.

Be Safe

Cook safely by having an adult around to help with these activities:

- Using a sharp knife or peeler
- Using the stove, microwave, blender, food processor, toaster, or other electrical appliances
- Removing hot pans from the oven (Always use pot holders.)
- Frying foods on top of the stove (Keep the heat as low as possible to avoid burns from oil splatter.)

Tools You Need

Many of the recipes in this book require a stove, refrigerator, toaster, or microwave oven. Most recipes also require four or five other common kitchen tools.*

Sharp knife	Ice cream scoop	Apple corer		Baking sheet	Small plate	Stove	Microwave
Butter knife	Scissors	Can opener		Small serving dish	Serving bowl and tray	Toaster	Pot holders
Paring knife	Spatula	Cutting board	Colander	Microwave-safe plate	Medium frying pan	Long toothpicks	3-ounce paper cups	Blender
Mixing spoon	Masher	Measuring spoons	Measuring cups	9" X 9" baking pan	Pot	Plastic wrap	1-gallon plastic sealable bag	Tall glass
Spoon	Small cookie cutters	Small bowl	Medium mixing bowl	Double boiler (or 2 pots, one that fits inside the other)		Aluminum foil	Wax paper
Wooden spoon							
Serving spoon							
Fork							

*If you do not have a particular tool, you can usually substitute another. For example, if you do not have a particular kind of knife or spoon—another kind will often work just fine.

Cheese and Fruit Kebabs

10 Minutes Prep Time

Tools

4 Servings

Ingredients

¼ pound cheese (cheddar, Monterey Jack, American, or any combination of the three)

1 cup assorted fresh fruit pieces (Choose your favorites!)

Steps

1. Ask an adult to use the knife to cut the cheese into 1- to 2-inch cubes on the cutting board. Or if you have small cookie cutters, press them into the cheese to make different shapes.

2. Take a long toothpick and slide the fruit and cheese onto it—one piece of cheese, followed by a piece of fruit, followed by a piece of cheese, and so on—to create a kebab.

3. Repeat Step 2 until 4 toothpicks are filled. Then enjoy your colorful work of art.

Health Tip

All types of fruits are high in vitamins and **minerals**.

Archaeologists have found the remains of what they think was cheese in Egyptian tombs that are more than 4,000 years old.

Quick Peanut Butter Bars

5 Minutes Prep Time*

Tools

15 Servings

*Plus 1 hour to cool

Ingredients

1 cup peanut butter

¾ cup honey

2 cups uncooked rolled oats

½ cup dried cranberries (or any dried fruit of your choice)

½ cup sunflower seeds (or other seeds or nuts of your choice)

Steps

1. Put the peanut butter and honey in the frying pan. With help from an adult, warm the ingredients over low heat on the stove top. Stir with the spoon until the ingredients are mixed and runny.

2. Stir in the oats, dried cranberries, and sunflower seeds until everything is nicely blended together.

3. Carefully pour the mixture into a 9" x 9" pan, using a spoon to help. Then, use the spatula to press it evenly into the pan.

4. Let the mixture cool for 1 hour and then ask an adult to cut it into 15 bars of equal size.

5. The bars do not need to be refrigerated. Just wrap them in aluminum foil. Grab one whenever you need a quick snack!

Americans eat about 500 million pounds of peanut butter every year—enough to cover the floor of the Grand Canyon!

9

Nutty Snack Mix

5 Minutes Prep Time

Tools

12 Servings

Health Tip

Not only are almonds tasty, they are also good for you when eaten in moderation. They're full of **vitamin E, fiber,** and heart-healthy fats.

Ingredients

4 cups whole nuts (at least 4 different types)

2 cups dried fruit (at least 4 different types)

1 cup small pretzel pieces or cereal (optional)

Steps

1. Pour all the nuts and dried fruit into the plastic bag.

2. If desired, add cereal or pretzel pieces.

3. Seal the bag carefully.

4. Shake the bag vigorously to mix everything up.

5. Pour some of the mixture into the bowl to enjoy. When you want a snack on the go, put some of the mixture in a small container or a plastic bag and take it with you.

As small as the sunflower seed is, it can produce a sunflower plant that is up to 12 feet tall.

Healthy Lemon Hummus

20 Minutes Prep Time

Tools

8 Servings

Ingredients

1 15-ounce can of chickpeas

⅓ cup lemon juice

1 tablespoon water

1 tablespoon olive oil

3 tablespoons peanut butter or **tahini**

¼ teaspoon garlic powder

Dash of salt

Vegetables washed and cut into strips or bite-size pieces (Choose your favorites!)

Pita bread, cut into small triangles

Steps

1. Use the can opener to open the can of chickpeas.

2. Put the colander in the sink and empty the can of chickpeas into it, allowing the liquid to drain. (Do not rinse the chickpeas.)

3. Pour the drained chickpeas into the blender.

4. Add the lemon juice, water, olive oil, peanut butter or tahini, garlic powder, and salt. Blend on high for 30 to 40 seconds, until smooth.

5. Pour the hummus from the blender into the serving bowl. Use the spoon to help.

6. Place the serving bowl in the middle of the serving tray. Arrange the vegetables and pita triangles around the bowl to use for dipping.

7. Use a few pieces of vegetables to create a funny face on the hummus. Serve and enjoy.

8. If you have leftover hummus, refrigerate it in a tightly covered container. It will keep for up to five days.

Hummus is the Arabic word for "chickpea."

Chick Peas

Frozen Fruit Pops

5
Minutes
Prep Time*

Tools

6
Servings

* Plus 1 to 2 hours freezing time

Ingredients

1 ½ cups fruit juice
(Use grape, orange,
or pineapple juice.)

½ cup fresh fruit cut into bite-size
pieces (You can use peaches,
pineapple, strawberries, or bananas.)

3 tall pretzel rods
(You can also use
6 Popsicle sticks.)

Steps

1. Pour ¼ cup of fruit juice into each of the six cups.

2. Add 1 tablespoon of fruit pieces to each cup.

3. Cover the tops of the paper cups with aluminum foil.

4. Break three pretzel rods in half.

5. Poke the broken end of a pretzel through the center of the aluminum foil covering each cup, making the pretzel stand straight up. If you don't want to use pretzels, poke a Popsicle stick through the center of the aluminum foil, making it stand up.

6. Put the cups in the freezer until the juice is frozen solid, about 1 to 2 hours.

7. When the juice is frozen, take off the foil and lay the pop on its side to peel off the paper cup. You may have to snip a little of the cup with scissors to get it started.

The average strawberry has more than 200 seeds.

Health Tip

Fruit is one of nature's wonder medicines because it is packed with vitamins, **minerals**, and **antioxidants**.

Cheese Tortilla with Salsa

3 Minutes Prep Time

Tools

2 Servings

Ingredients

1 tortilla

½ cup grated cheese (Use your favorite.)

½ cup salsa

Steps

1. Place the tortilla on a microwave-safe plate.

2. Sprinkle the cheese in the middle of the tortilla and fold it in half.

3. With help from an adult, microwave the tortilla and cheese for 30 seconds or until the cheese melts.

4. Using pot holders, carefully take the hot plate out of the microwave.

5. Slice the tortilla into wedges on the cutting board.

6. Spoon salsa into the small dish. Dip the warm cheese triangles into the salsa and enjoy.

The United States is the largest producer of cheese in the world, with the states of Wisconsin and California making the most. However, people in Greece and France eat more cheese per person than people in the United States.

Party Pretzels

10 Minutes Prep Time*

*Plus 1 hour freezing time

Tools (4) (or more)

12 Servings

Ingredients

About ½ cup of your favorite toppings (You can use one or more of the following: chocolate chips, shredded coconut, sprinkles, chopped nuts, or sunflower seeds.)

1 cup flavored yogurt (A thick yogurt, such as Greek yogurt, works best.)

12 pretzel rods or pretzel sticks

Steps

1. Line a baking sheet with wax paper.

2. Put each topping onto its own small plate.

3. Put the yogurt on a plate.

4. Roll each pretzel in the yogurt so that at least half the pretzel stick is covered.

5. Hold the pretzel over one topping plate. Use your fingers or a small spoon to sprinkle the topping on the part of the pretzel covered in yogurt. Rotate the pretzel so all sides are covered.

6. Place the pretzel on the wax paper.

7. After decorating all the pretzels, put the baking sheet in the freezer for one hour before enjoying!

Until the 1930s, pretzels were handmade and usually twisted into loops. The average worker could twist 40 pretzels a minute. In 1935, a pretzel machine was invented. It could make 245 pretzels per minute.

Health Tip

Try using **low-fat** Greek yogurt instead of regular yogurt. Greek yogurt tends to contain more **protein** than the regular kind.

Bug Parade

Tools

Health Tip

Celery has very few **calories** and contains **vitamin A, vitamin C, iron, calcium**, and lots of **fiber**.

Ingredients

2 tall celery stalks or 2 firm bananas

About ⅓ cup filling of your choice (You can use Greek yogurt, Neufchâtel cheese, peanut butter, cottage cheese, and so on.)

About 2 tablespoons small dried fruit (Try dried cranberries, raisins, cherries, or any dried fruit of your choice.)

Steps

1. Wash the celery. Ask an adult to use the paring knife to cut the stalks into 4-inch strips. If you are using bananas, peel them, cut them in half, and then slice each half down the middle.

2. With the butter knife, spread your favorite filling into the groove of each celery stick or on the long flat sides of the banana pieces.

3. Place the dried fruit in a line on top of the filling.

4. Enjoy the bug parade!

The ancient Greeks only used celery as a medicine. They believed it calms the nerves. It wasn't until the 1700s that celery was eaten as a food.

Chocolate-Dipped Fruit

About 1 Hour Prep Time*

Tools

8 Servings

*Plus 15 minutes to refrigerate

Ingredients

Water

1 tablespoon butter

1 cup chocolate chips

About 10 large, washed strawberries with the stems on

3 firm bananas, peeled and cut into pieces

1 pear, washed and cut into pieces (You can also use apple, mango, or melon.)

Steps

1. Put water into the bottom pot of the double boiler and place it on the stove top. With help from an adult, turn on the heat to bring the water to a **boil**. Once it starts boiling, turn down the heat to let the water **simmer**.

2. Carefully set the top pot inside the pot with the simmering water. Put the butter in this pot to melt. Then add the chocolate chips and stir with a wooden spoon until the mixture is smooth and blended.

3. Turn off the heat. Using pot holders, carefully move the double boiler to a heat resistant surface.

4. Put the wax paper on the baking sheet.

5. Hold a strawberry by the stem and dip the other end into the melted mixture. Then hold it over the pot to let the extra chocolate drip off. Place the strawberry on the waxed sheet.

6. Repeat Step 5 with the other strawberries and fruit pieces. It may help to use a toothpick to dip some kinds of fruit.

7. Put the baking sheet of chocolate-dipped fruit in the refrigerator to set for 15 minutes. Then enjoy!

Make these snacks the same day you plan to eat them. Store leftovers in a sealed container in the refrigerator for up to two days. Although bananas may start to brown within a day, they are still tasty.

Apple Puzzle

10 Minutes Prep Time

Tools

2 Servings

Ingredients

1 firm, washed apple that stands upright (Granny Smith apples work well.)

¼ cup peanut butter

2 tablespoons chopped walnuts (If you don't want to use walnuts, you can use coconut, grated carrot, shredded cheddar cheese, raisins, or other toppings of your choice.)

Steps

1. Ask an adult to **core** the apple using either an apple corer or a knife. Then slice the apple into thin rounds (¼- to ½-inch thick) on the cutting board.

2. Using the butter knife, spread each apple slice with peanut butter.

3. Sprinkle walnuts or other toppings on the slices.

4. Reassemble the apple, putting the pieces on top of each other.

5. Share with a friend, each taking one apple slice at a time.

Health Tip

Always eat the skin with the rest of the apple. It contains lots of **vitamin C, fiber,** and other **nutrients**.

The largest apple ever picked weighed about three pounds—about the same weight as a half gallon of milk.

Great Guacamole Dip

15
Minutes
Prep Time

Tools

8
Servings

Ingredients

2 avocados

2 tablespoons lemon juice

¼ cup sour cream

1 small tomato (about ½ cup chopped tomato)

2 green onions

½ teaspoon garlic powder

Salt to taste

About 4 cups of assorted vegetables, washed and cut into small pieces

Steps

1. Ask an adult to use the knife to cut the avocados in half on the cutting board. Remove the pit from each avocado and throw it away. With the spoon, scrape out the green fleshy part of the fruit from the rind and put it in the mixing bowl.

2. Add the lemon juice to the avocado. Then mash the avocado flesh with the masher.

3. Mix in the sour cream with the spoon, blending it well.

4. Cut the tomato and green onions into little pieces. If the tomato is too juicy, put the colander in the sink and drain the pieces.

5. Add the tomato and onion to the avocado mixture and stir gently.

6. Stir in the garlic powder and salt.

7. Spoon the guacamole into a serving bowl. Place it in the center of the serving tray. Spread vegetables around the bowl for dipping. Use a few vegetables to make a face on the guacamole.

One avocado tree can produce between 150 and 500 avocados a year.

Deviled Egg Delights

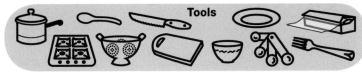
Tools

*Plus 30 minutes cooling time and 30 minutes refrigerator time

12 Servings

Ingredients

6 eggs

Water

2 tablespoons mayonnaise

1 teaspoon milk

1 teaspoon Dijon mustard

Salt and pepper to taste

A dash of paprika

Steps

1. Carefully place the eggs in the bottom of a large pot. There should be a little space between each egg. Cover the eggs with water. With an adult's help, bring the water to a boil on the stove top. Then lower the heat and let the eggs **simmer** for 15 minutes.

2. Place the colander in the sink. Carefully remove each boiled egg from the pot with a large spoon and place in the colander. Run cold water over the eggs. Then let them cool for 30 minutes.

3. Crack the shells of the cool eggs and gently peel them off. Then cut each egg in half lengthwise on the cutting board.

4. Pop out the yolk from each egg half. They come out easily. Just hold the side with the yolk over a bowl and pull back on the ends of the egg. Put the white egg halves on a plate.

5. Add the mayonnaise, milk, and mustard to the yolks. Mash them with the fork until the ingredients are blended and there aren't any lumps. The mixture will be firm. Add salt and pepper to taste.

6. Fill the yolk space in each egg half with a teaspoon of filling from the bowl.

7. Sprinkle the filled eggs with paprika. Cover them with plastic wrap and refrigerate at least 30 minutes. Serve when chilled.

Health Tip

Don't leave eggs out of the refrigerator for more than an hour or so, particularly in hot weather. They will spoil.

Most hens lay about 245 eggs per year.

Pizza Bites

Not only do tomatoes taste good, they are also good for you. They are chock-full of important vitamins, such as **vitamin A** and **vitamin C**.

10 Minutes Prep Time

Tools

2 Servings

Ingredients

1 English muffin

3 tablespoons tomato sauce

2 tablespoons shredded mozzarella cheese

1 tablespoon vegetables, washed and cut into small pieces (For example, you can use cut-up zucchini, red bell pepper, or mushrooms.)

Steps

1. Split open the English muffin and toast the halves until light brown.

2. Put the halves on a microwave-safe plate. Then spoon 1 ½ tablespoons of sauce onto each toasted muffin half, spreading it evenly.

3. Using your fingers, sprinkle cheese on top of the sauce.

4. Sprinkle the vegetables on top of the cheese.

5. With an adult's help, heat the pizzas in the microwave for 40 seconds or until the cheese melts.

6. Using pot holders, carefully take the plate out of the microwave. Cut each little pizza into halves or quarters so that you can share with a friend.

Pizza **means "pie" in Italian. The women of Naples, Italy, created pizzas more than 300 years ago.**

Yogurt, Granola, and Fruit Creations

5 Minutes Prep Time

Tools

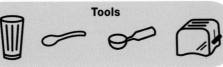

1 Serving

Ingredients

1 cup yogurt or frozen yogurt

½ cup granola

Cut-up fresh fruit of your choice (You can use blueberries, strawberries, melon, watermelon, mangos, peaches, etc.)
- ½ cup for waffle or tall glass
- 1½ cups for cone

Waffle cone

Waffle

Steps

For a tall glass:

1. With a spoon, layer the yogurt, granola, and fruit in a tall glass.

For a cone:

1. Use the spoon to put the cut-up fruit in the waffle cone.

2. Top the fruit with a scoop of yogurt and sprinkle with granola.

For a waffle:

1. Toast the waffle and then top with a scoop of yogurt. Add fruit for decoration and sprinkle with granola.

Health Tip

Yogurt is a great source of **protein** as well as **calcium**.

Yogurt got its name from the Turkish word *yogurur*, which means "long life."

Healthy Tips

Always Read Labels

Labels tell how much fat, sugar, vitamins, and other nutrients are in food. If you compare one bottle of juice with another, for example, you can determine which one has fewer **calories**, less sugar, and so on.

Make Recipe Substitutions

While all the recipes in this book call for wholesome ingredients, you can make even healthier snacks by substituting some ingredients for others. For example:

 Dairy—Use non-fat or **low-fat** instead of full-fat when it comes to dairy products, such as yogurt, frozen yogurt, cheese, sour cream, and milk.

Bread—Choose pita bread, English muffins, or tortillas that are 100 percent whole wheat.

Salt—Choose "lightly salted" or "no salt added" nuts to reduce **sodium** content.

Juice—Choose 100 percent fruit juice with no added sugar.

Cereal—Choose cereal that is low in sugar and fat and high in fiber.

Glossary

antioxidants (*an*-tee-OK-suh-duhnts) substances found in certain foods that may prevent cell damage, which can cause disease in people and animals

archaeologists (*ar*-kee-OL-uh-jists) scientists who learn about ancient times by studying things they dig up, such as old buildings, tools, and pottery

boil (BOIL) when a liquid is heated up to the point that it bubbles

calcium (KAL-see-uhm) a chemical element found in vegetables, milk, and milk products; it's important for the growth and maintenance of strong bones and teeth

calories (KAL-uh-reez) measurements of the amount of energy that food provides

core (KOR) to take out the center of a piece of fruit

fiber (FYE-bur) a substance found in parts of plants that when eaten passes through the human body without being completely digested; because it helps food move through the intestines, it is very important for good health

iron (EYE-urn) a mineral found in foods such as meat, eggs, dried fruit and certain vegetables; it helps move oxygen from the lungs to the rest of the body

low-fat (loh-FAT) food that has three or fewer grams of fat per serving

minerals (MIN-ur-uhlz) chemical substances, such as iron or zinc, that occur naturally in certain foods and are important for good health

nutrients (NOO-tree-uhnts) proteins, vitamins, fats, and other things in food that are needed to stay healthy

obesity (oh-BEESS-uh-tee) a condition in which a person is extremely overweight

preservatives (pri-ZUR-vuh-tivz) chemicals that are added to food so that it won't spoil

protein (PROH-teen) a substance found in plants and animals that provides energy to the body; it can be found in cheese, yogurt, eggs, fish, meat, beans, and other foods

simmer (SIM-ur) to boil slowly at a low temperature

sodium (SOH-dee-uhm) a chemical found in salt that the body needs in small amounts; too much salt in one's diet can cause health problems

tahini (tuh-HEE-nee) a sesame seed paste

vitamin A (VYE-tuh-min AY) a type of vitamin found in tomatoes, sweet potatoes, spinach, and other foods; helps preserve and improve eyesight

vitamin C (VYE-tuh-min SEE) a type of vitamin found in fruits and vegetables; it's important for healing the body and for keeping teeth and bones strong

vitamin E (VYE-tuh-min EE) a type of vitamin found in whole grains and vegetable oils; it helps protect a person's cells and tissues from damage

vitamin K (VYE-tuh-min KAY) a type of vitamin found in milk, yogurt, and certain green vegetables; it helps a wounded person's blood to clot

Index

Bibliography

Julien, Ronni. *What Should I Feed My Kids? How to Keep Your Children Healthy by Teaching Them to Eat Right.* Franklin Lakes, NJ: New Page Books (2006).

Trice, Laura. *The Wholesome Junk Food Cookbook: More Than 100 Healthy Recipes for Everyday Snacking.* Philadelphia: Running Press (2010).

Read More

Warner, Penny. *Healthy Snacks for Kids.* Hayward, CA: Bristol Pub. Enterprises (2007).

Wilensky, Amy. *Healthy Snacks for Kids: Recipes for Nutritious Bites at Home or On the Go.* Guilford, CT: Knack (2010).

Learn More Online

To learn more about making artful snacks, visit
www.bearportpublishing.com/YummyTummyRecipes

About the Author

Marilyn LaPenta has been a teacher for more than 25 years and has published numerous works for teachers and students. She has always enjoyed cooking with her students, her three children, and her three grandchildren. Marilyn lives in Brightwaters, New York, with her husband, Philip.